500 Motivating and Inspiring Quotes

Discovering Great Leaders and People

Nigel Aksel

1ˢᵗ Edition

Published in Amazon.com

Nigel Aksel
500 Motivating and Inspiring Quotes: Discovering Great Leaders and People

1st Edition
All Rights Reserved
ISBN: 9781687341495

Table of Content

Dedication

This book is prepared for my children, who are so curious to learn about new ideas and especially of great leaders of our planet.

These quotes are motivating and inspiring and they lead anyone to many ideas and actions. And I hope that anyone can benefit from using these quotes and find new ways to resolve own life issues or achieve cherished goals with a totally new vision of the great people.

Enjoy your reading!

Best wishes,

Nigel Aksel

Action

1. "The way to get started is to quit talking and begin doing." -Walt Disney
2. "Success seems to be connected with action. Successful people keep moving. They make mistakes but they don't quit." -Conrad Hilton
3. "Twenty years from now you will be more disappointed by the things that you didn't do than by the ones you did do. So, throw off the bowlines, sail away from safe harbor, catch the trade winds in your sails. Explore, Dream, Discover." -Mark Twain
4. "Start where you are. Use what you have. Do what you can." -Arthur Ashe
5. "People ask, 'What's the best role you've ever played?' The next one." -Kevin Kline
6. "If you want to achieve excellence, you can get there today. As of this second, quit doing less-than-excellent work." -Thomas J. Watson

7. "Keep on going, and the chances are that you will stumble on something, perhaps when you are least expecting it. I never heard of anyone ever stumbling on something sitting down." -Charles F. Kettering
8. "Don't be too timid and squeamish about your actions. All life is an experiment. The more experiments you make the better." -Ralph Waldo Emerson
9. "Don't judge each day by the harvest you reap but by the seeds that you plant." -Robert Louis Stevenson
10. "Pearls don't lie on the seashore. If you want one, you must dive for it." -Chinese proverb
11. "The best time to plant a tree was 20 years ago. The second best time is now." -Chinese Proverb
12. "A ship in harbor is safe, but that is not what ships are built for." -John A. Shedd
13. "Be content to act, and leave the talking to others." -Baltasar Gracian

14. "If your ship doesn't come in,
swim out to meet it!" -Jonathan
Winters
15. "Doubt is only removed by action.
If you're not working then that's
where doubt comes in." -Conor
McGregor

Belief

16. "Believe you can and you're halfway there." -Theodore Roosevelt
17. "You become what you believe." -Oprah Winfrey
18. "You can't connect the dots looking forward; you can only connect them looking backward. So you have to trust that the dots will somehow connect in your future. You have to trust in something - your gut, destiny, life, karma, whatever. This approach has never let me down, and it has made all the difference in my life." -Steve Jobs

19. "To me, business isn't about wearing suits or pleasing stockholders. It's about being true to yourself, your ideas and focusing on the essentials." - Richard Branson
20. "A ship in harbor is safe, but that is not what ships are built for." - John A. Shedd
21. "The entrepreneur builds an enterprise; the technician builds a job." -Michael Gerber
22. "A real entrepreneur is somebody who has no safety net underneath them." -Henry Kravis
23. "Most new jobs won't come from our biggest employers. They will come from our smallest. We've got to do everything we can to make entrepreneurial dreams a reality." -Ross Perot
24. "My son is now an 'entrepreneur'. That's what you're called when you don't have a job." -Ted Turner
25. "Going into business for yourself, becoming an entrepreneur, is the modern-day equivalent of

pioneering on the old frontier." -
Paula Nelson

26. "Nobody talks of entrepreneurship
    as survival, but that's exactly what
    it is." -Anita Roddick
27. "The best reason to start an
    organization is to make meaning;
    to create a product or service to
    make the world a better place." -
    Guy Kawasaki
28. "Make your product easier to buy
    than your competition, or you will
    find your customers buying from
    them, not you." -Mark Cuban
29. "If you don't have a competitive
    advantage, don't compete." -Jack
    Welch
30. "The individual who wants to
    reach the top in business must
    appreciate the might and force of
    habit. He must be quick to break
    those habits that can break him
    and hasten to adopt those
    practices that will become the
    habits that help him achieve the
    success he desires." -J. Paul
    Getty
31. "A business that makes nothing
    but money is a poor business." -
    Henry Ford

32. "A business has to be involving, it has to be fun, and it has to exercise your creative instincts." - Richard Branson
33. "If you're competitor-focused, you have to wait until there is a competitor doing something. Being customer-focused allows you to be more pioneering." -Jeff Bezos

34. "Do not go where the path may lead, go instead where there is no path and leave a trail." -Ralph Waldo Emerson

35. "I've missed more than 9000 shots in my career. I've lost almost 300 games. 26 times I've been trusted to take the game-winning shot and missed. I've failed over and over and over again in my life. And that is why I succeed." -Michael Jordan

36. "Never underestimate the power you have to take your life in a new direction." -Germany Kent

37. "I never dreamed about success. I worked for it." -Estee Lauder

38. "Work to become, not to acquire." -Elbert Hubbard

39. "Choose a job you love, and you will never have to work a day in your life." -Confucius

40. "Your career is like a garden. It can hold an assortment of life's energy that yields a bounty for you. You do not need to grow just one thing in your garden. You do not need to do just one thing in your career." - Jennifer Ritchie Payette

Change

41. "It is not the strongest of the species that survive, nor the most intelligent, but the one most responsive to change." -Charles Darwin
42. "Change will not come if we wait for some other person or some other time. We are the ones we've been waiting for. We are the change that we seek." -Barack Obama
43. "If you want to make a permanent change, stop focusing on the size of your problems and start focusing on the size of you!" -T. Harv Eker
44. "Every great dream begins with a dreamer. Always remember, you have within you the strength, the patience, and the passion to reach for the stars to change the world." -Harriet Tubman
45. "If you have no will to change it, you have no right to criticize it." -Mark Twain
46. "When the winds of change blow, some people build walls and

others build windmills." -Chinese Proverb

47. "The secret of change is to focus all of your energy, not on fighting the old, but on building the new." -Socrates

Courage

48. "Success is not final; failure is not fatal: It is the courage to continue that counts." -Winston S. Churchill
49. "Don't be afraid to give up the good to go for the great." -John D. Rockefeller
50. "It often requires more courage to dare to do right than to fear to do wrong." -Abraham Lincoln
51. "Often the difference between a successful person and a failure is not one has better abilities or ideas, but the courage that one has to bet on one's ideas, to take a calculated risk and to act." - André Malraux
52. "All our dreams can come true if we have the courage to pursue them." -Walt Disney

Creativeness

53. "Curiosity about life in all of its aspects, I think, is still the secret of great creative people." -Leo Burnett
54. "Don't think. Thinking is the enemy of creativity. It's self-conscious, and anything self-conscious is lousy. You can't try to do things. You simply must do things." -Ray Bradbury
55. "Creativity is just connecting things. When you ask creative people how they did something, they feel a little guilty because they didn't really do it, they just saw something. It seemed obvious to them after a while." -Steve Jobs
56. "Think before you speak is criticism's motto; speak before you think, creation's." -E. M. Forster
57. "Creativity is a natural extension of our enthusiasm." -Earl Nightingale

Criticism

58. "Don't be distracted by criticism.
    Remember - the only taste of
    success some people get is to
    take a bite out of you." -Zig Ziglar
59. "There is only one way to avoid
    criticism: do nothing, say nothing,
    and be nothing." -Aristotle
60. "I am thankful for all of those who
    said NO to me. It's because of
    them I'm doing it myself." -Albert
    Einstein
61. "You can't blame gravity for falling
    in love." -Albert Einstein
62. "If we judge ourselves only by our
    aspirations and everyone else
    only by their conduct, we shall
    soon reach a very false
    conclusion." -Calvin Coolidge
63. "When we speak evil of others,
    we generally condemn
    ourselves." -Publius Syrus
64. "The critic has to educate the
    public; the artist has to educate
    the critic." -Oscar Wilde
65. "A creative life cannot be
    sustained by approval any more
    than it can be destroyed by
    criticism." -Will Self

66. "When men speak ill of thee, live so as nobody may believe them." -Plato

67. "The individual must not merely wait and criticize, he must defend the cause the best he can. The fate of the world will be such as the world deserves." -Albert Einstein

68. "Whatever you do, you need courage. Whatever course you decide upon, there is always someone to tell you that you are wrong. There are always difficulties arising that tempt you to believe your critics are right." - Ralph Waldo Emerson

69. "Don't criticize what you don't understand, son. You never walked in that man's shoes." - Elvis Presley

70. "If someone criticizes you, give them a compliment." -Debasish Mridha

71. "Any fool can criticize, complain, and condemn--and most fools do. But it takes character and self-control to be understanding and forgiving." -Dale Carnegie

72. "Criticism is information that will help you grow." -Hendrie Weisinger
73. "All my life, people have said that I wasn't going to make it." -Ted Turner
74. "I like criticism. It makes you strong." -LeBron James
75. "Criticism may not be agreeable, but it is necessary. It fulfills the same function as pain in the human body. It calls attention to an unhealthy state of things." -Winston Churchill
76. "While we would love to have no criticism, probably if we had no critique, we wouldn't be doing anything meaningful." -Erwin McManus

Discipline

77. "Anyone who has ever made anything of importance was disciplined." -Andrew Hendrixson
78. "Success in business requires training and discipline and hard work. But if you're not frightened by these things, the opportunities are just as great today as they ever were." -David Rockefeller
79. "Discipline is the bridge between goals and accomplishment." -Jim Rohn
80. "Discipline is the soul of an army. It makes small numbers formidable; procures success to the weak, and esteem to all." -George Washington
81. "A disciplined mind leads to happiness, and an undisciplined mind leads to suffering." -Dalai Lama
82. "The only discipline that lasts is self-discipline." -Bum Philips
83. "Discipline is the refining fire by which talent becomes ability." -Roy L. Smith

84. "With self-discipline, most anything is possible." -Theodore Roosevelt

85. "If I want to be great I have to win the victory over myself…self-discipline." -Harry S. Truman

86. "I could only achieve success in my life through self-discipline, and I applied it until my wish and my will became one." -Nikola Tesla

87. "Self-command is the main discipline." -Ralph Waldo Emerson

88. "Without self-discipline, success is impossible, period." -Lou Holtz

89. "He who lives without discipline dies without honor." -Icelandic Proverb

90. "The price of excellence is discipline. The cost of mediocrity is disappointment." -William Arthur Ward

91. "Self-discipline is the No.1 delineating factor between the rich, the middle class, and the poor." -Robert Kiyosaki

92. "Confidence comes from discipline and training." -Robert Kiyosaki

93. "Success doesn't just happen. You have to be intentional about it, and that takes discipline." -John C. Maxwell
94. "No man is fit to command another that cannot command himself." -William Penn
95. "Self-control is the chief element in self-respect, and self-respect is the chief element in courage." -Thucydides
96. "Success is nothing more than a few simple disciplines, practiced every day." -Jim Rohn
97. "By constant self-discipline and self-control you can develop greatness of character." -Grenville Kleiser
98. "Self-discipline is about controlling your desires and impulses while staying focused on what needs to get done to achieve your goal." -Adam Sicinski
99. "The more disciplined you become, the easier life gets." -Steve Pavlina
100. "We don't have to be smarter than the rest; we have to be more disciplined than the rest." -Warren Buffett

101.	"Never believe a promise from a man or woman who has no discipline. They have broken a thousand promises to themselves, and they break their promise for you." -Matthew Kelly
102.	"Self control is the key to self esteem and self confidence." -Laurance McGraw V
103.	"No life ever grows great until it is focused, dedicated, disciplined." -Harry Emerson Fosdick
104.	"I think self-discipline is something, it's like a muscle. The more you exercise it, the stronger it gets." -Daniel Goldstein
105.	"Self-discipline is the magic power that makes you virtually unstoppable." -Dan Kennedy
106.	"It doesn't matter whether you are pursuing success in business, sports, the arts, or life in general: The bridge between wishing and accomplishing is discipline." -Harvey Mackay
107.	"Mastering others is strength. Mastering yourself is true power." -Lao Tzu

Doubts

108.   "The only limit to our realization of tomorrow will be our doubts of today." -Franklin D. Roosevelt

109.   "If you're offered a seat on a rocket ship, don't ask what seat! Just get on." -Sheryl Sandberg

110.   "Do the one thing you think you cannot do. Fail at it. Try again. Do better the second time. The only people who never tumble are those who never mount the high wire. This is your moment. Own it." -Oprah Winfrey

111.   "It is better to keep your mouth closed and let people think you are a fool than to open it and remove all doubt." -Mark Twain

112.   "Never doubt that a small group of thoughtful, committed citizens can change the world; indeed, it's the only thing that ever has." -Margaret Mead

113.   "Inaction breeds doubt and fear. Action breeds confidence and courage. If you want to conquer fear, do not sit home and

think about it. Go out and get busy." -Dale Carnegie

114.   "Never let self-doubt hold you captive." -Roy Bennett

115.   "Successful people have fear, successful people have doubts, and successful people have worries. They just don't let these feelings stop them." -T. Harv Eker

116.   "Great leaders are almost always great simplifiers, who can cut through argument, debate and doubt, to offer a solution everybody can understand." -Colin Powell

117.   "I've learned that the mastery of self-doubt is the key to success." -Will Smith

118.   "I love it when people doubt me. It makes me work harder to prove them wrong." -Derek Jeter

119.   "Don't ever doubt yourselves or waste a second of your life. It's too short, and you're too special." -Ariana Grande

120.   "Doubt kills more dreams than failure ever will." -Suzy Kassem

Dream and Think

121.   "Dream big and dare to fail." -Norman Vaughan

122.   "Dreaming, after all, is a form of planning." -Gloria Steinem

123.   "Twenty years from now you will be more disappointed by the things that you didn't do than by the ones you did do. So, throw off the bowlines, sail away from safe harbor, catch the trade winds in your sails. Explore, Dream, Discover." -Mark Twain

124.   "All our dreams can come true if we have the courage to pursue them."- Walt Disney

125.   "When you cease to dream you cease to live." -Malcolm Forbes

126.   "A dream doesn't become reality through magic; it takes sweat, determination, and hard work." -Colin Powell

127.   "Everything you can imagine is real." -Pablo Picasso

128.   "But you have to do what you dream of doing even while you're afraid." -Arianna Huffington

129.   "If you don't build your dream, someone else will hire you to help them build theirs." - Dhirubhai Ambani

130.   "Think big and don't listen to people who tell you it can't be done. Life is too short to think small." -Tim Ferriss

131.   "Too many of us are not living our dreams because we are living our fears." -Les Brown

132.   "As long as you're going to be thinking anyway, think big." - Donald Trump

133.   "Logic will get you from A to B. Imagination will take you everywhere." -Albert Einstein

Enemy

134.   "Always forgive your enemies; nothing annoys them so much." -Oscar Wilde

135.   "You have enemies? Good. That means you've stood up for something sometime in your life." -Winston Churchill

136.   "Ideas are more powerful than guns. We would not let our enemies have guns, why should we let them have ideas." -Joseph Stalin

137.   "The art of war teaches us to rely not on the likelihood of the enemy's not coming, but on our own readiness to receive him; not on the chance of his not attacking, but rather on the fact that we have made our position unassailable." -Sun Tzu

138.   "A man who was completely innocent, offered himself as a sacrifice for the good of others, including his enemies, and became the ransom of the world. It was a perfect act." -Mahatma Gandhi

139.   "Anger and intolerance are the enemies of correct understanding." -Mahatma Gandhi

140.   "Be loyal to those who are loyal to you. And respect everyone, even your enemies and competition." -John Cena

141.   "I have lots of friends, but I'm probably a terrible friend to all of them, even my family. I wouldn't be surprised if I found myself with no friends later on in life. My friends become my enemies." -Ariel Pink

142.   "War is the remedy that our enemies have chosen, and I say let us give them all they want." -William Tecumseh Sherman

143.   "If you don't have enemies, you don't have character." -Paul Newman

Enthusiasm

144.   "Nothing great was ever achieved without enthusiasm." -Ralph Waldo Emerson

145.   "Flaming enthusiasm, backed up by horse sense and persistence, is the quality that most frequently makes for success." -Dale Carnegie

146.   "Success is walking from failure to failure with no loss of enthusiasm." -Winston Churchill

147.   "Enthusiasm is the mother of effort, and without it nothing great was ever achieved." -Ralph Waldo Emerson

148.   "I consider my ability to arouse enthusiasm among men the greatest asset I possess. The way to develop the best that is in a man is by appreciation and encouragement." -Charles Schwab

149.   "I believe that education is all about being excited about something. Seeing passion and enthusiasm helps push an educational message." -Steve Irwin

150.   "Enthusiasm is the yeast that makes your hopes shine to the stars. Enthusiasm is the sparkle in your eyes, the swing in your gait. The grip of your hand, the irresistible surge of will and energy to execute your ideas." - Henry Ford

Failure

151.   "The real test is not whether you avoid this failure, because you won't. It's whether you let it harden or shame you into inaction, or whether you learn from it; whether you choose to persevere." -Barack Obama

152.   "The road to success and the road to failure are almost exactly the same." -Colin R. Davis

153.   "It is better to fail in originality than to succeed in imitation." -Herman Melville

154.   "There are no secrets to success. It is the result of preparation, hard work, and learning from failure." -Colin Powell

155.   "Success is walking from failure to failure with no loss of enthusiasm." -Winston Churchill

156.   "Dream big and dare to fail." -Norman Vaughan

157.   "You may be disappointed if you fail, but you are doomed if you don't try." -Beverly Sills

158.	"I didn't fail the test. I just found 100 ways to do it wrong." - Benjamin Franklin

159.	"I have not failed. I've just found 10,000 ways that won't work." - Thomas Edison

160.	"Failure is another steppingstone to greatness." - Oprah Winfrey

161.	"Don't worry about failure; you only have to be right once." - Drew Houston

162.	"Failure defeats losers, failure inspires winners." -Robert T. Kiyosaki

163.	"The No. 1 reason people fail in life is because they listen to their friends, family, and neighbors." -Napoleon Hill

Fear

164.   "Everything you've ever wanted is on the other side of fear." -George Addair

165.   "Too many of us are not living our dreams because we are living our fears." -Les Brown

166.   "I have learned over the years that when one's mind is made up, this diminishes fear." -Rosa Parks

167.   "Do one thing every day that scares you." -Eleanor Roosevelt

168.   "Our greatest fear should not be of failure... but of succeeding at things in life that don't really matter." -Francis Chan

169.   "Successful people have fear, successful people have doubts, and successful people have worries. They just don't let these feelings stop them." -T. Harv Eker

170.   "Keep your fears to yourself, but share your courage with others." -Robert Louis Stevenson

171.   "There is no easy walk to freedom anywhere, and many of us will have to pass through the valley of the shadow of death again and again before we reach the mountaintop of our desires." -Nelson Mandela

172.   "The freedom to do your best means nothing unless you are willing to do your best." -Colin Powell

173.   "The link between my experience as an entrepreneur and that of a politician is all in one word: freedom." -Silvio Berlusconi

174.   "The greatest threat to freedom is the absence of criticism." -Wole Soyinka

175.   "True freedom is impossible without a mind made free by discipline." -Mortimer J. Adler

176.   "Discipline without freedom is tyranny. Freedom without discipline is chaos." -Cullen Hightower

Friendship

177. "A friendship founded on business is a good deal better than a business founded on friendship." -John D. Rockefeller

178. "A friend is someone who gives you total freedom to be yourself." -Jim Morrison

179. "One measure of friendship consists not in the number of things friends can discuss, but in the number of things they need no longer mention." -Clifton Fadiman

180. "Friendship is delicate as a glass, once broken it can be fixed but there will always be cracks." -Waqar Ahmed

181. "Be slow to fall into friendship, but when you are in, continue firm and constant." -Socrates

182. "Do I not destroy my enemies when I make them my friends?" -Abraham Lincoln

183. "Friendship marks a life even more deeply than love. Love risks degenerating into obsession, friendship is never anything but sharing." -Elie Wiesel

Goals

184. "If you set your goals ridiculously high and it's a failure, you will fail above everyone else's success." -James Cameron

185. "Don't judge each day by the harvest you reap but by the seeds that you plant." -Robert Louis Stevenson

186. "The future belongs to those who believe in the beauty of their dreams." -Eleanor Roosevelt

187. "The only person you are destined to become is the person you decide to be." -Ralph Waldo Emerson

188. "First, have a definite, clear practical ideal; a goal, an objective. Second, have the necessary means to achieve your ends; wisdom, money, materials, and methods. Third, adjust all your means to that end." -Aristotle

189. "A goal is a dream with a deadline." -Napoleon Hill

190. "People are not lazy. They simply have important goals – that is, goals that do not inspire them." -Tony Robbins

Happiness

191.   "Whoever is happy will make others happy too." -Anne Frank

192.   "Happiness is a butterfly, which when pursued, is always beyond your grasp, but which, if you will sit down quietly, may alight upon you." -Nathaniel Hawthorne

193.   "I refuse to accept other people's ideas of happiness for me. As if there's a one size fits all standard for happiness." -Kanye West

194.   "Happiness is when what you think, what you say, and what you do are in harmony." -Mahatma Gandhi

195.   "If you want to live a happy life, tie it to a goal, not to people or objects." -Albert Einstein

Hard work

196.   "I find that the harder I work, the more luck I seem to have." -Thomas Jefferson

197.   "There are no secrets to success. It is the result of preparation, hard work, and learning from failure." -Colin Powell

198.   "Keep your face to the sunshine and you can never see the shadow." -Helen Keller

199.   "Rarely have I seen a situation where doing less than the other guy is a good strategy." -Jimmy Spithill

200.   "Every day I get up and look through the Forbes list of the richest people in America. If I'm not there, I go to work." -Vinnie Rege

201.   "Success in business requires training and discipline and hard work. But if you're not frightened by these things, the opportunities are just as great today as they ever were." -David Rockefeller

202.   "The three great essentials
to achieve anything worthwhile
are, first, hard work; second,
stick-to-itiveness; third, common
sense." -Thomas A. Edison

Hope

203.   "Learn from yesterday, live for today, hope for tomorrow. The important thing is not to stop questioning." -Albert Einstein

204.   "Once you choose hope, anything's possible." -Christopher Reeve

205.   "Never lose hope. Storms make people stronger and never last forever." -Roy T. Bennett

206.   "We must accept finite disappointment, but never lose infinite hope." -Martin Luther King

207.   "A person can do incredible things if he or she has enough hope." -Shannon K. Butcher

208.   "Hope can be a powerful force. Maybe there's no actual magic in it, but when you know what you hope for most and hold it like a light within you, you can make things happen, almost like magic." -Laini Taylor

209.   "Hope is a waking dream." -Aristotle

210.   "There is a saying in Tibetan, 'Tragedy should be utilized as a source of strength.'

No matter what sort of difficulties, how painful experience is, if we lose our hope, that's our real disaster." -Dalai Lama XIV

211.	"Plant seeds of happiness, hope, success, and love; it will all come back to you in abundance. This is the law of nature." -Steve Maraboli

212.	"Hope can get you through anything." -Jamie Ford

213.	"The best way to not feel hopeless is to get up and do something. Don't wait for good things to happen to you. If you go out and make some good things happen, you will fill the world with hope, you will fill yourself with hope." -Barack Obama

214.	"Hope keeps you alive." - Lauren Olive

Innovation

215. "Innovation distinguishes between a leader and a follower." -Steve Jobs

216. "Innovation comes from saying NO to 1,000 things." - Steve Jobs

217. "Innovation has nothing to do with how many R & D dollars you have. When Apple came up with the Mac, IBM was spending at least 100 times more on R & D. It's not about money. It's about the people you have, how you're led, and how much you get it." - Steve Jobs

218. "Without change there is no innovation, creativity, or incentive for improvement. Those who initiate change will have a better opportunity to manage the change that is inevitable." -William Pollard

219. "Software innovation, like almost every other kind of innovation, requires the ability to collaborate and share ideas with other people, and to sit down and talk with customers and get their

feedback and understand their needs." -Bill Gates

220.	"I think frugality drives innovation, just like other constraints do. One of the only ways to get out of a tight box is to invent your way out." -Jeff Bezos

221.	"Innovation is taking two things that already exist and putting them together in a new way." -Tom Freston

222.	"Innovation is the central issue in economic prosperity." - Michael Porter

223.	"Trust the young people; trust this generation's innovation. They're making things, changing innovation every day. And all the consumers are the same: they want new things, they want cheap things, they want good things, they want unique things. If we can create these kind of things for consumers, they will come." -Jack Ma

Investment

224.   "An investment in knowledge pays the best interest." -Benjamin Franklin

225.   "Bottoms in the investment world don't end with four-year lows; they end with 10- or 15-year lows." -Jim Rogers

226.   "In investing, what is comfortable is rarely profitable." -Robert Arnott

227.   "Invest in yourself. Your career is the engine of your wealth." -Paul Clitheroe

228.   "The individual investor should act consistently as an investor and not as a speculator." -Ben Graham

229.   "I would not pre-pay. I would invest instead and let the investments cover it." -Dave Ramsey

230.   "Wide diversification is only required when investors do not understand what they are doing." -Warren Buffett

231.   "Buy when everyone else is selling and hold until everyone else is buying. That's not just a

catchy slogan. It's the very essence of successful investing." -J. Paul Getty

232.	"How many millionaires do you know who have become wealthy by investing in savings accounts? I rest my case." - Robert G. Allen

233.	"Investment is most successful when it is most businesslike." -Ben Graham

234.	"To be a successful business owner and investor, you have to be emotionally neutral to winning and losing. Winning and losing are just part of the game." - Rich Dad

235.	"My two rules of investing: Rule one - never lose money. Rule two - never forget rule one." -Warren Buffett

236.	"The rich invest in time, the poor invest in money." -Warren Buffett

Leadership

237.   "If your actions inspire others to dream more, learn more, do more, and become more, you are a leader." -John Quincy Adams

238.   "As we look ahead into the next century, leaders will be those who empower others." -Bill Gates

239.   "The function of leadership is to produce more leaders, not more followers." -Ralph Nader

240.   "One of the criteria for national leadership should therefore be a talent for understanding, encouraging, and making constructive use of vigorous criticism." -Carl Sagan

241.   "Great leaders always have self-discipline -without exception." -John C. Maxwell

242.   "Leadership is not about titles, positions, or flowcharts. It is about one life influencing another." -John C. Maxwell

243.   "Leadership is an action, not a position." -Donald McGannon

Learning

244.   "Tell me and I forget. Teach me and I remember. Involve me and I learn." - Benjamin Franklin

245.   "There are no secrets to success. It is the result of preparation, hard work, and learning from failure." -Colin Powell

246.   "I've learned that people will forget what you said, people will forget what you did, but people will never forget how you made them feel." -Maya Angelou

247.   "I have learned over the years that when one's mind is made up, this diminishes fear." -Rosa Parks

248.   "Learn from yesterday, live for today, hope for tomorrow. The important thing is not to stop questioning." -Albert Einstein

249.   "Live as if you were to die tomorrow. Learn as if you were to live forever." -Mahatma Gandhi

250.   "When you take risks you learn that there will be times when you succeed and there will be

times when you fail, and both are equally important." -Ellen DeGeneres

251. "Success in business requires training and discipline and hard work. But if you're not frightened by these things, the opportunities are just as great today as they ever were." -David Rockefeller

252.   "If life were predictable it would cease to be life, and be without flavor." -Eleanor Roosevelt

253.   "The greatest glory in living lies not in never falling, but in rising every time we fall." -Nelson Mandela

254.   "The way to get started is to quit talking and begin doing." -Walt Disney

255.   "If you look at what you have in life, you'll always have more. If you look at what you don't have in life, you'll never have enough." -Oprah Winfrey

256.   "Life is what happens when you're busy making other plans." -John Lennon

257.   "The best and most beautiful things in the world cannot be seen or even touched - they must be felt with the heart." -Helen Keller

258.   "The best and most beautiful things in the world cannot be seen or even touched - they must be felt with the heart." -Helen Keller

259.	"You will face many defeats in life, but never let yourself be defeated." -Maya Angelou

260.	"In the end, it's not the years in your life that count. It's the life in your years." -Abraham Lincoln

261.	"Life is either a daring adventure or nothing at all." -Helen Keller

262.	"Life is really simple, but we insist on making it complicated." -Confucius

263.	"Life is a long lesson in humility." -James M. Barrie

264.	"Life itself is the most wonderful fairy tale." -Hans Christian Andersen

265.	"Love the life you live. Live the life you love." -Bob Marley

266.	"Life is ours to be spent, not to be saved." -D. H. Lawrence

267.	"Keep smiling, because life is a beautiful thing and there's so much to smile about." -Marilyn Monroe

268.	"In three words I can sum up everything I've learned about life: it goes on." -Robert Frost

269.	"Life is made of ever so many partings welded together." -Charles Dickens

270.	"An unexamined life is not worth living." -Socrates

271.	"Life is 10% what happens to me and 90% of how I react to it." -Charles Swindoll

272.	"Nothing is impossible, the word itself says, 'I'm possible!'" -Audrey Hepburn

273.	"When everything seems to be going against you, remember that the airplane takes off against the wind, not with it." -Henry Ford

274.	"Learn from yesterday, live for today, hope for tomorrow. The important thing is not to stop questioning." -Albert Einstein

275.	"The longer I live, the more beautiful life becomes." -Frank Lloyd Wright

276.	"I believe every human has a finite number of heartbeats. I don't intend to waste any of mine." -Neil Armstrong

277.	"The two most important days in your life are the day you are born and the day you find out why." -Mark Twain

278.	"As you grow older, you will discover that you have two hands, one for helping yourself, the other for helping others." -Audrey Hepburn

279.	"The more you praise and celebrate your life, the more there is in life to celebrate." -Oprah Winfrey

280.	"We become what we think about most of the time, and that's the strangest secret." -Earl Nightingale

281.	"Life is short, and it is here to be lived." -Kate Winslet

282.	"I don't want to get to the end of my life and find that I lived just the length of it. I want to have lived the width of it as well." -Diane Ackerman

283.	"If you don't design your own life plan, chances are you'll fall into someone else's plan. And guess what they have planned for you? Not much." -Jim Rohn

284.	"You don't choose your family. They are God's gift to you, as you are to them." -Desmond Tutu

285.	"It is impossible to escape the impression that people commonly use false standards of measurement - that they seek power, success and wealth for themselves and admire them in others, and that they underestimate what is of true value in life." -Sigmund Freud

286.	"If life were predictable it would cease to be life, and be without flavor." -Eleanor Roosevelt

287.	"You're not obligated to win. You're obligated to keep trying. To the best you can do everyday." -Jason Mraz

288.	"In order to write about life first you must live it." -Ernest Hemingway

289.	"I only regret that I have but one life to give for my country." -Nathan Hale

290.	"Every child is an artist, the problem is staying an artist when you grow up." -Pablo Picasso

291.	"Life is not a problem to be solved, but a reality to be experienced." -Søren Kierkegaard

292.   "Spread love everywhere
you go. Let no one ever come to
you without leaving happier." -
Mother Teresa

293.   "The best and most
beautiful things in the world
cannot be seen or even touched -
they must be felt with the heart." -
Helen Keller

294.   "Love the life you live. Live
the life you love." -Bob Marley

295.   "Your work is going to fill a
large part of your life, and the only
way to be truly satisfied is to do
what you believe is great work.
And the only way to do great work
is to love what you do. If you
haven't found it yet, keep looking.
Don't settle. As with all matters of
the heart, you'll know when you
find it." -Steve Jobs

296.   "If you love what you do
and are willing to do what it takes,
it's within your reach. And it'll be
worth every minute you spend
alone at night, thinking and
thinking about what it is you want

to design or build." -Steve Wozniak

297.   "I never knew how to worship until I knew how to love." -Henry Ward Beecher

298.   "To love and be loved is to feel the sun from both sides." -David Viscott

299.   "Love is an irresistible desire to be irresistibly desired." -Robern Frost

300.   "Better to have loved and lost, than to have never loved at all." -St. Augustine

Luck

301.   "I find that the harder I work, the more luck I seem to have." -Thomas Jefferson

302.   "Remember that sometimes not getting what you want is a wonderful stroke of luck." -Dalai Lama XIV

303.   "I've found that luck is quite predictable. If you want more luck, take more chances. Be more active. Show up more often." -Brian Tracy

304.   "Luck never gives; it only lends." -Swedish Proverb

305.   "When luck is on your side it is not the time to be modest or timid. It is the time to go for the biggest success you can possibly achieve." -Donald Trump

306.   "Luck is what happens when preparation meets opportunity." -Seneca

Markets

307.   "You get recession, you have stock market declines. If you don't understand that's going to happen, then you're not ready, you won't do well in the markets."
-Peter Lynch

308.   "The stock market is a device for transferring money from the impatient to the patient."
-Warren Buffett

309.   "In the short run, the market is a voting machine. But in the long run, it is a weighing machine." -Ben Graham

310.   "Stock market bubbles don't grow out of thin air. They have a solid basis in reality, but reality as distorted by a misconception." -George Soros

311.   "Stop trying to predict the direction of the stock market, the economy or the elections." -Warren Buffett

312.   "The markets generally are unpredictable, so that one has to have different scenarios. The idea that you can actually predict what's going to happen

contradicts my way of looking at the market." -George Soros

313.	"Historically, there has been a bull market in the commodities every 20 or 30 years." -Jim Rogers

314.	"Look at market fluctuations as your friend rather than your enemy. Profit from folly rather than participate in it." -Warren Buffett

Mind

315. "Whatever the mind of man can conceive and believe, it can achieve." -Napoleon Hill

316. "First, have a definite, clear practical ideal; a goal, an objective. Second, have the necessary means to achieve your ends; wisdom, money, materials, and methods. Third, adjust all your means to that end." -Aristotle

317. "Great minds discuss ideas; average minds discuss events; small minds discuss people." - Eleanor Roosevelt

318. "Don't limit yourself. Many people limit themselves to what they think they can do. You can go as far as your mind lets you. What you believe, remember, you can achieve." -Mary Kay Ash

319. "I avoid looking forward or backward, and try to keep looking upward." -Charlotte Bronte

320. "In the midst of movement and chaos, keep stillness inside of you." -Deepak Chopra

321. "The person who reads too much and uses his brain too little

will fall into lazy habits of
thinking." -Albert Einstein

322.   "A disciplined mind leads to
happiness, and an undisciplined
mind leads to suffering." -Dalai
Lama

Mistakes

323.   "Success seems to be connected with action. Successful people keep moving. They make mistakes but they don't quit." -Conrad Hilton

324.   "Success does not consist in never making mistakes but in never making the same one a second time." -George Bernard Shaw

325.   "Show me a person who has never made a mistake and I'll show you someone who has never achieved much." -Joan Collins

326.   "Even a mistake may turn out to be the one thing necessary to a worthwhile achievement." -Henry Ford

327.   "Only those who are asleep make no mistakes." -Ingvar Kamprad

Money

328.   "First, have a definite, clear practical ideal; a goal, an objective. Second, have the necessary means to achieve your ends; wisdom, money, materials, and methods. Third, adjust all your means to that end." -Aristotle

329.   "I will tell you how to become rich. Close the doors. Be fearful when others are greedy. Be greedy when others are fearful." -Warren Buffet

330.   "Poor people have a big TV. Rich people have big library." -Jim Rohn

331.   "Big pay and little responsibility are circumstances seldom found together." -Napoleon Hill

332.   "Stop chasing the money and start chasing the passion." -Tony Hsieh

333.   "It's not how much money you make, but how much money you keep, how hard it works for you, and how many generations you keep it for." -Robert Kiyosaki

334.   "Too many people spend money they earned.to buy things they don't want.to impress people that they don't like." -Will Rogers

335.   A wise person should have money in their head, but not in their heart. -Jonathan Swift

336.   "Money often costs too much." -Ralph Waldo Emerson

337.   "The Stock Market is designed to transfer money from the Active to the Patient." -Warren Buffett

338.   "When buying shares, ask yourself, would you buy the whole company?" -Rene Rivkin

339.   "I never attempt to make money on the stock market. I buy on assumption they could close the market the next day and not re-open it for five years." -Warren Buffett

Motivation

340.   "In my experience, there is only one motivation, and that is desire. No reasons or principle contain it or stand against it." - Jane Smiley

341.   "People often say that motivation doesn't last. Well, neither does bathing – that's why we recommend it daily." -Zig Ziglar

342.   "Only those who attempt the absurd can achieve the impossible." -Albert Einstein

343.   "Motivation gets you going, but discipline keeps you growing." -John C. Maxwell

344.   "When a man is sufficiently motivated, discipline will take care of itself." -Albert Einstein

Opportunity

345.   "Opportunities don't happen. You create them." -Chris Grosser

346.   "To be successful, you must accept all challenges that come your way. You can't just accept the ones you like." -Mike Gafka

347.   "Saying it is impossible to live without failing at something is impossible. Unless you live so cautiously that you might as well not have lived at all, in which case you have failed by default." -J.K. Rowling

348.   "Leap and the net will appear." -Zen Proverb

349.   "Don't worry about failures, worry about the chances you miss when you don't even try." -Jack Canfield

350.   "When one door of happiness closes, another opens; but often we look so long at the closed door that we do not see the one which has been opened for us." -Helen Keller

351.   "Opportunity is missed by most people because it is dressed in overalls and looks like work." - Thomas Edison
352.   "Where victims see adversity, extreme achievers see opportunity." -Robin Sharma
353.   "Opportunities are rarely offered; they're seized." -Sheryl Sandberg
354.   "If you believe it will work out, you'll see opportunities. If you believe it won't, you will see obstacles." -Wayne Dyer

Pace

355.   "It does not matter how slowly you go as long as you do not stop." -Confucius

356.   "If things seem under control, you are just not going fast enough." -Mario Andretti

357.   "Without continual growth and progress, such words as improvement, achievement, and success have no meaning." -Benjamin Franklin

358.   "Your greatest and most powerful business survival strategy is going to be the speed at which you handle the speed of change. That speed of change is trend." -Ajaero Tony Martins

359.   "I would rather die of passion than of boredom." -Vincent van Gogh

360.   "Always go with your passions. Never ask yourself if it's realistic or not." -Deepak Chopra

361.   "There is no passion to be found playing small - in settling for a life that is less than the one you are capable of living." -Nelson Mandela

362.   "Nothing great in the world has ever been accomplished without passion." -George Hegel

363.   "Without passion, you don't have energy, without energy you have nothing." -Donald Trump

364.   "The very basic of a man's living spirit is his passion for adventure." -Christopher McCandless

365.   "Passion will move men beyond themselves, beyond their shortcomings, beyond their failures." -Joseph Campbell

366.   "To succeed you have to believe in something with such

passion that it becomes a reality."
-Anita Roddick
367.	"True passion attracts. If
you have passion in your
business, the right people will be
attracted to your team." -Robert T.
Kiyosaki
368.	"Dreams and passion are
more powerful than facts and
reality." -Gail Lynne Goodwin

369. "Always remember that you are absolutely unique. Just like everyone else." -Margaret Mead

370. "Be yourself. Everyone else is already taken." -Oscar Wilde

371. "Be patient with yourself. Self-growth is tender; it's holy ground. There's no greater investment." -Stephen Covey

372. "It is never too late to be what you might have been." -George Eliot

373. "I don't think you're human if you don't get nervous." -Sidney Crosby

374. "If you cannot do great things, do small things in a great way." -Napoleon Hill

375. "Poor people have a big TV. Rich people have big library." -Jim Rohn

376. "Nearly all men can stand adversity, but if you want to test a man's character, give him power." -Abraham Lincoln

377. "Identify your problems but give your power and energy to solutions." -Tony Robbins

378. "You have power over your mind, not outside events. Realize this, and you will find strength." -Marcus Aurelius

379. "Most powerful is he who has himself in his own power." -Seneca

380. Self-control is strength, right thought is mastery, calmness is power." -James Allen

381. "Mastering others is strength. Mastering yourself is true power." -Lao Tzu

382. "What it lies in our power to do, it lies in our power not do." -Aristotle

Responsibility

383.   "Big pay and little responsibility are circumstances seldom found together." -Napoleon Hill

384.   "The price of greatness is responsibility" -Winston Churchill

385.   "Happiness will come to you when it comes from you. Success will be yours when you choose to take responsibility for making it so." -Ralph Marston

386.   "Responsibility to yourself means refusing to let others do your thinking, talking, and naming for you; it means learning to respect and use your own brains and instincts; hence, grappling with hard work." -Adrienne Rich

387.   "The choices we make are ultimately our responsibility." -Eleanor Roosevelt

388.   "Responsibility finds a way. Irresponsibility makes excuses!" -Gene Bedley

389.   "We have a responsibility to help those around us and help others in need." -Virginia Williams

Risk

390.   "If you are not willing to risk the usual, you will have to settle for the ordinary." -Jim Rohn

391.   "The biggest risk is not taking any risk... In a world that's changing really quickly, the only strategy that is guaranteed to fail is not taking risks." -Mark Zuckerberg

392.   "Only those who will risk going too far can possibly find out how far one can go." -T. S. Eliot

393.   "Only those who play to win. Only those who risk to win. History favors risk-takers. Forgets the timid. Everything else is commentary." -Iveta Cherneva

394.   "And the day came when the risk to remain tight in a bud was more painful than the risk it took to blossom." -Anais Nin

395.   "Life is inherently risky. There is only one big risk you should avoid at all costs, and that is the risk of doing nothing." -Denis Waitley

Stubbornness

396.   "If you're not stubborn, you'll give up on experiments too soon. And if you're not flexible, you'll pound your head against the wall and you won't see a different solution to a problem you're trying to solve." -Jeff Bezos

397.   "Being stubborn has helped, being selfish is not a bad thing." -Herbie Mann

398.   "A man will do more for his stubbornness than for his religion or his country." -E. W. Howe

399.   "Smallness of mind is the cause of stubbornness, and we do not credit readily what is beyond our view." -Francois de la Rochefoucauld

400.   "Stubbornness is the strength of the weak." -Johann Kaspar Lavater

401.   "Being stubborn can be a good thing. Being stubborn can be a bad thing. It just depends on how you use it." -Willie Aames

402.   "Before anything else, preparation is the key to success." -Alexander Graham Bell

403.   "Success is the sum of small efforts, repeated day-in and day-out." -Robert Collier

404.   "Many of life's failures are people who did not realize how close they were to success when they gave up." -Thomas A. Edison

405.   "Success usually comes to those who are too busy to be looking for it." -Henry David Thoreau

406.   "The way to get started is to quit talking and begin doing." -Walt Disney

407.   "The secret of success is to do the common thing uncommonly well." -John D. Rockefeller Jr.

408.   "A successful man is one who can lay a firm foundation with the bricks others have thrown at him." -David Brinkley

409.	"The road to success and the road to failure are almost exactly the same." -Colin R. Davis

410.	"Successful people do what unsuccessful people are not willing to do. Don't wish it were easier; wish you were better." -Jim Rohn

411.	"There are no secrets to success. It is the result of preparation, hard work, and learning from failure." -Colin Powell

412.	"Success seems to be connected with action. Successful people keep moving. They make mistakes but they don't quit." -Conrad Hilton

413.	"I never dreamed about success, I worked for it." -Estee Lauder

414.	"Don't be distracted by criticism. Remember - the only taste of success some people get is to take a bite out of you." -Zig Ziglar

415.	"Try not to become a man of success. Rather become a man of value." -Albert Einstein

416. "Always bear in mind that your own resolution to success is more important than any other one thing." -Abraham Lincoln

417. "Success is walking from failure to failure with no loss of enthusiasm." -Winston Churchill

418. "You know you are on the road to success if you would do your job and not be paid for it." -Oprah Winfrey

419. "People who succeed have momentum. The more they succeed, the more they want to succeed and the more they find a way to succeed. Similarly, when someone is failing, the tendency is to get on a downward spiral that can even become a self-fulfilling prophecy." -Tony Robbins

420. "Winning isn't everything, but wanting to win is." -Vince Lombardi

421. "I attribute my success to this: I never gave or took any excuse." -Florence Nightingale

422. "Someone is sitting in the shade today because someone planted a tree a long time ago." -Warren Buffett

423.   "Whenever you see a successful person, you only see the public glories, never the private sacrifices to reach them." - Vaibhav Shah

424.   "Success? I don't know what that word means. I'm happy. But success, that goes back to what in somebody's eyes success means. For me, success is inner peace. That's a good day for me." -Denzel Washington

425.   "The best revenge is massive success." -Frank Sinatra

426.   "The whole secret of a successful life is to find out what is one's destiny to do, and then do it." -Henry Ford

427.   "The distance between insanity and genius is measured only by success." -Bruce Feirstein

428.   "All progress takes place outside the comfort zone." - Michael John Bobak

429.   "You may only succeed if you desire succeeding; you may only fail if you do not mind failing." -Philippos

430.   "The first step toward success is taken when you refuse

to be a captive of the environment in which you first find yourself." - Mark Caine

431.	"The successful warrior is the average man, with laser-like focus." -Bruce Lee

432.	"Success is most often achieved by those who don't know that failure is inevitable." - Coco Chanel

433.	"Often the difference between a successful person and a failure is not one has better abilities or ideas, but the courage that one has to bet on one's ideas, to take a calculated risk and to act." -André Malraux

434.	"Success is a lousy teacher. It seduces smart people into thinking they can't lose." -Bill Gates

435.	"What is success? I think it is a mixture of having a flair for the thing that you are doing; knowing that it is not enough, that you have got to have hard work and a certain sense of purpose." - Margaret Thatcher

Teamwork

436.   "Remember, teamwork begins by building trust. And the only way to do that is to overcome our need for invulnerability." - Patrick Lencioni

437.   "Alone, we can do so little; together, we can do so much." - Helen Keller

438.   "Individual commitment to a group effort: That is what makes a team work, a company work, a society work, a civilization work." - Vince Lombardi

439.   "None of us is as smart as all of us." -Ken Blanchard

440.   "Talent wins games, but teamwork and intelligence win championships." -Michael Jordan

441.   "Teamwork is the ability to work together toward a common vision, the ability to direct individual accomplishments toward organizational objectives. It is the fuel that allows common people to attain uncommon results." -Andrew Carnegie

442.   "If everyone is moving forward together, then success takes care of itself." -Henry Ford

443.   "I'm not the smartest fellow in the world, but I sure can pick smart colleagues." -Franklin D Roosevelt

444.   "Individually, we are one drop. Together, we are an ocean." -Ryunosuke Satoro

445.   "No matter how brilliant your mind or strategy, if you're playing a solo game, you'll always lose out to a team." -Reid Hoffman

446.   "Building a mission and building a business go hand in hand." -Mark Zuckerberg

447.   "The speed of the boss is the speed of the team." -Lee Iacocca

Time

448.   "Your time is limited, so don't waste it living someone else's life. Don't be trapped by dogma – which is living with the results of other people's thinking." -Steve Jobs

449.   "It is never too late to be what you might have been." -George Eliot

450.   "Time is what we want most, but what we use worst." -William Penn

451.   "Time = life; therefore, waste your time and waste of your life, or master your time and master your life." -Alan Lakein

452.   "The key is in not spending time, but in investing it." -Stephen R. Covey

453.   "A man who dares to waste one hour of life has not discovered the value of life." -Charles Darwin

454.   "Take care of the minutes and the hours will take care of themselves." -Lord Chesterfield

455.   "To do two things at once is to do neither." -Publius Syrus

456. "One cannot manage too many affairs: like pumpkins in the water, one pops up while you try to hold down the other." -Chinese Proverb

457. "The time for action is now. It's never too late to do something." -Carl Sandburg

458. "Money, I can only gain or lose. But time I can only lose. So, I must spend it carefully." -Old Proverb

459. "Time is money." -Benjamin Franklin

460. "Gaining time is gaining everything in love, trade and war." -John Shebbeare

461. "Your greatest resource is your time." -Brian Tracy

462. "Time is at once the most valuable and the most perishable of all our possessions." -John Randolph

463. "Until we can manage time, we can manage nothing else." -Peter F. Drucker

464. "You may delay, but time will not." -Benjamin Franklin

465. "Don't say you don't have enough time. You have exactly the

same number of hours per day that were given to Helen Keller, Pasteur, Michelangelo, Mother Teresa, Leonardo da Vinci, Thomas Jefferson, and Albert Einstein." -H. Jackson Brown

466.	"The bad news is time flies. The good news is you're the pilot." -Michael Altshuler

467.	"Time is the coin of your life. It is the only coin you have, and only you can determine how it will be spent. Be careful lest you let other people spend it for you." -Carl Sandburg

468.	"The great dividing line between success and failure can be expressed in five words: "I did not have time." -Franklin Field

Understanding

469.	"If you can't explain it simply, you don't understand it well enough."
-Albert Einstein

470.	"Identity is a prison you can never escape, but the way to redeem your past is not to run from it, but to try to understand it, and use it as a foundation to grow." -Jay-Z

471.	"If we listened to our intellect, we'd never have a love affair. We'd never have a friendship. We'd never go into business because we'd be too cynical. Well, that's nonsense. You've got to jump off cliffs all the time and build your wings on the way down." -Annie Dillard

472.	"Everybody is a genius. But if you judge a fish by its ability to climb a tree, it will live its whole life believing that it is stupid." -Albert Einstein

473.	"The big lesson in life, baby, is never be scared of anyone or anything." -Frank Sinatra

474.   "Anger and intolerance are the enemies of correct understanding." -Mahatma Gandhi

Vision

475. "Capital isn't scarce; vision is." -Sam Walton

476. "I've been blessed to find people who are smarter than I am, and they help me to execute the vision I have." -Russell Simmons

477. "Vision is the art of seeing the invisible." -Jonathan Swift

478. "If you don't have a vision you're going to be stuck in what you know. And the only thing you know is what you've already seen." -Iyanla Vanzant

479. "Vision without action is merely a dream. Action without vision just passes the time. Vision with action can change the world." -Joel A. Barker

480. "Leadership is the capacity to translate vision into reality." -Warren G. Bennis

481. "A dream is the creative vision for your life in the future." -Denis Waitley

482. "Vision is the true creative rhythm." -Robert Delaunay

483.   "Champions aren't made in the gyms. Champions are made from something they have deep inside them – a desire, a dream, a vision." -Muhammad Ali

484.   "Microsoft was founded with a vision of a computer on every desk, and in every home. We've never wavered from that vision." -Bill Gates

485.   "If you are working on something exciting that you really care about, you don't have to be pushed. The vision pulls you." -Steve Jobs

486.   "Vision without execution is hallucination." -Thomas Edison

487.   "I alone cannot change the world, but I can cast a stone across the water to create many ripples." -Mother Teresa

488.   "How wonderful it is that nobody need wait a single moment before starting to improve the world." -Anne Frank

489.   "There are two types of people who will tell you that you cannot make a difference in this world: those who are afraid to try and those who are afraid you will succeed."-Ray Goforth

490.   "The universe has no restrictions. You place restrictions on the universe with your expectations." -Deepak Chopra

491.   "When you undervalue what you do, the world will undervalue who you are." -Oprah Winfrey

492.   "It is far better to be alone, than to be in bad company." - George Washington

493.   "What good is an idea if it remains an idea? Try. Experiment. Iterate. Fail. Try

again. Change the world." -Simon Sinek

494.   "Never doubt that a small group of thoughtful, committed citizens can change the world. Indeed, it is the only thing that ever has." -Margaret Mead

495.   "Be the change that you wish to see in the world." - Mahatma Gandhi

496.   "Education is the most powerful weapon which you can use to change the world." -Nelson Mandela

497.   "Taking a new step, uttering a new word, is what people fear most." -Fyodor Dostoyevsky

498.   "I wanted to change the world. But I have found that the only thing one can be sure of changing is oneself." -Aldous Huxley

499.   "Things changed, people changed, and the world went rolling along right outside the window." -Nicholas Sparks

500.   "Change your thoughts and you change your world." -Norman Vincent Peale

Conclusion

This was my first try where I collected all quotes of great leaders and people in one book.

I very hope that it will benefit my readers as a tool for motivation and inspiration.

I will be happy to see your comments and ideas about how I can improve my next editions of the book. I also welcome any think tank projects, where I can participate and contribute to resolving important issues of today's motivation of people for achieving great goals.

Feel free send me your message or your comment via email at nurbek2002@yahoo.com

About author

Nigel Aksel is a professional expert with more than 20 years of experience in market research. From 2018, he is involved as a lecturer of marketing and management at the South-Kazakhstan State University.

Nigel enjoys writing about multiple issues of education, science, learning, and other related topics. As a member of various institutions, he understands well about the problems of global education, illiteracy, and development. He explores many areas of the economy on how to make learning more effective for economic and social development.

Notes and Memories

Where can you find interesting stories about investments, export, and trade on the internet?

Nurbek Achilov has some resources for you!

On Blogger's platform, he runs his blog about investments, export, trade, and other issues.

Blog about investment, export, and trade in English:

https://nurbekachilov.blogspot.com/

Blog about investment, export, and trade in English:

https://nurbekachil.blogspot.com/

You can also find ideas, photos, and experiences about investments, trade and investment on Nurbek Achilov's pages on Facebook, Instagram, Pinterest, Slideshare,

Academia and LinkedIn and other accounts.

orcid.org/0000-0003-1238-6556

Kazakhstan

Tips for Travelers

Nurbek Achilov

Second Edition

200 web-sites and tools for online presence

Essential Handbook for marketing and growth

Nurbek Achilov

First Edition

Event Management

Tips and strategies

Nigel Aksel

Second Edition

Order my newest book with the Special
Price on Amazon.com

Global Citizen

Thinking Beyond

Nurbek Achilov

First Edition

Greenification

Develop, Educate and Promote

Nurbek Achilov

First Edition

Market Trends

Historical Data

Nigel Aksel

Second Edition